Join Us

S0-ASC-344

Jill Bever and Sheilah Currie

One and one makes two.

2 children

One and two makes three.

3 teddy bears

Three and two makes five.

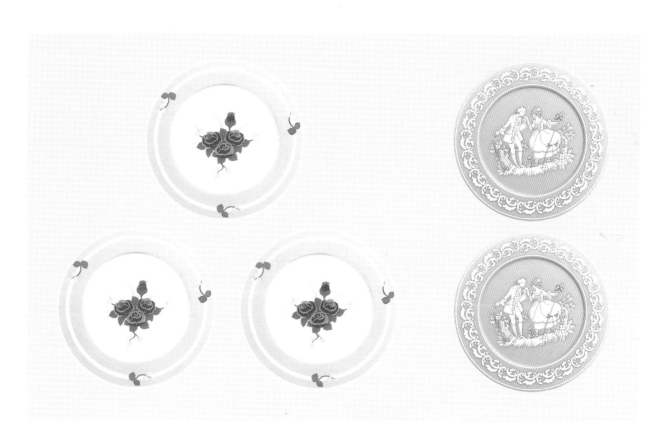

5 plates

Two and three makes five.

5 mugs

Five and one makes six.

6 spoons

Five and five makes ten.

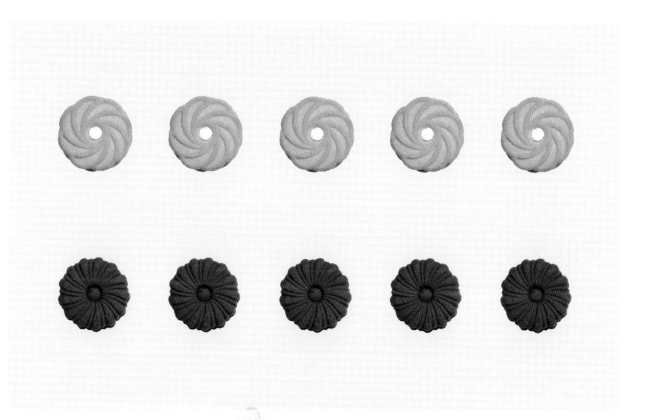

10 cookies

Six and three makes nine.

9 flowers

It's a tea party!